My Father's Love

My Father's Love

DAVID BRAY

RESOURCE *Publications* · Eugene, Oregon

MY FATHER'S LOVE

Resource Publications
An Imprint of Wipf and Stock Publishers
199 W. 8th Ave., Suite 3
Eugene, OR 97401
www.wipfandstock.com

ISBN 13: 978-1-61097-589-6
Manufactured in the U.S.A.

I dedicate this book to the memory of my dad, John Bray.
Many people have helped me along my rocky road to maturity.
To all those folks who loved me unconditionally,
prayed for me without giving up,
and who encouraged me daily,
I also dedicate this book.

Contents

A Word of Background
for the Reader

WHEN THE writer of this testimony to his father's love, David Bray, was three and a half years old, a psychiatrist diagnosed him as "developmentally delayed" and expected he would have to be institutionalized by the time he reached puberty. But his parents nurtured him in their home and equipped him to get as much education as possible: David graduated from high school and completed a year of Bible college. His father—John Bray, a pastor, teacher, and dean of North Park Seminary—never looked down on David for his disabilities, but encouraged him, helped him deal with his emotions, found creative ways to give him opportunities to learn and grow and gain the maximum independence as a young man. He is legally disabled due to various mental and psychological symptoms, alleviated by medication. Prayer, counsel, and the caring folks at JPUSA combine to help David manage his limitations. Contrary to that childhood prognosis, David has now worked for over ten years at a tee shirt company owned and operated by JPUSA and lives semi-independently as a contributing member of that community.

This simple story of a father's love for his son will encourage any father or anyone struggling with the loss of a father or loved one. It offers concrete examples of positive relationships for any family and especially for families with a disabled child. David's memories of his dad demonstrate the power of love and radiate hope for those in grief, those with disabilities, families of the disabled, and any father or child needing reassurance of God's love.

Introduction

S OME DADS are pretty cool. I was fortunate to have a great dad. He was a positive role model for me, someone in whose footsteps I wanted to follow. I was proud of him and it has been my goal to become like him. He was my best friend. I am sure there are some of you who do not have great dads. But even if you don't have a wonderful earthly father, you can still find comfort and love from another "father," God.

My dad passed away in November 2000. It has been a heartache and a struggle dealing with my loss and loneliness. Dad was my hero. When I was feeling down, he would encourage me. When I was happy, he shared in my joy. Dad was able to understand me even when I was not completely able to express myself. For example, when I would come home from school, angry and wanting "to kill my bullies," Dad would help me to understand that my feelings had been hurt but that I really didn't want to eliminate those kids.

Dad never looked down on me because of my disabilities. He wished that I didn't have to struggle with learning. If he had been able, he would have taken away my limitations and taken them onto himself. Instead, he encouraged me and reminded me of Romans 8:28, which says that God works everything out for good for those who love him and are called according to his purpose and plan. We don't see the good in the midst of our struggles. But, in looking back, we are able to see where God has helped. I have been told that because of the disabilities, I have had to work harder than most students do in order to achieve success. I was persistent and I didn't give up. I have a capacity for understanding and acceptance towards other people that I wouldn't have had if I had been born without my handicaps.

My father put in extra effort to encourage us as his family. He felt that God had put us together for a purpose. Other families dealing with disabilities saw our family as an example of how to trust God in the midst of struggles. Were our spirits always positive? No! We were ordinary human beings who had the good fortune to be supported by the extraordinary support and love of Christian friends.

This book is written to encourage those of you who have lost your dad. Losing my dad almost destroyed me. I remember the night before he died, I told him how much I loved and admired him. That is my last memory of talking with him. I miss my dad, especially on holidays and on the anniversary of his death. While I miss him, I know that he is in a better place.

It is wonderful being a Christian. I and my brothers and sisters in Christ have hope beyond our own deaths. When one of us dies, it isn't the end but a passing from this life into a richer life in the presence of God. Now we see through a glass darkly, but someday we will see him face to face. That is God's promise and our hope. We will also be reunited with our loved ones.

My desire is that you will find hope and be blessed by reading my story. I dedicate this book to the memory of my father, John Bray. Many people have helped me along my rocky road to maturity. To all those folks who loved me unconditionally, prayed for me without giving up, and who encouraged me daily, I also dedicate this book.

1

"Happy Days"

M Y CLOSE relationship with my dad began at an early age. When I was just two weeks old, I developed Pyloric Stenosis, a condition in which the valve between the throat and the stomach closes. This is a genetic condition that occurs more often in males. My dad had had the same condition and almost died from it.

Pyloric Stenosis didn't allow my food to pass from my throat into my stomach. Projectile vomiting was the result, as the food had nowhere to go. I wasn't getting any benefit from my feedings. I was starving and losing weight. My first doctor thought that my mom was describing normal spitting up. But there wasn't anything normal about my vomiting! I was like an upended milk bottle, crying for more milk.

The next morning, Dad took me to another, younger doctor who diagnosed the problem right away after learning that I wasn't voiding any urine. I was operated on that same day and recovered rapidly. All that was needed was to clip the pyloric valve so that an opening was made for food to pass into my stomach. I have had no further problem—maybe too much good food and ample gut! During my hospital stay, my dad held and comforted me, dangling tubes and all. My tired but relieved mom went home to sleep. Years later she told me that she had feared that I was going to die.

When I was only three years old, Dad would come tiptoeing to my door, quietly open it and come over to my bed. Whispering, he would ask me if I wanted to watch *Star Trek* with him. To this day, my favorite DVDs are old *Star Trek* movies. I own and play the movie sound tracks and collect all kinds of *Star Trek* memorabilia. I have attended several Trekkie conventions, bought autographs of some of the original cast members and have a Starfleet uniform. I am a hopeless "Trekkie"! Other shows that Dad and I watched together were *Happy Days*, *Mission Impossible*, and *All in the Family*.

I have many other happy memories. One day, Dad dressed me up in his suit vest and tie. Lugging his briefcase into the kitchen, I declared to Mom that I was leaving for work. My mom treasures pictures of me dressed like that. My buddy, Sean, and I spent hours playing dress up. One day, we came up with a combo old grannie/Michael Jackson outfit, each of us wearing curly gray wigs and sharing a pair of white gloves. The wigs were courtesy of some ladies in the church.

Every Saturday, Dad and I would go out for breakfast at Bob's Big Boy restaurant. We lived in Salina, Kansas, at the time. Whenever we went there, a waitress named Janet served us. She was my first "love" as a kid. We had a McDonalds near our house. This restaurant had a big American flag out in front. In those days, I had a fixation on flags, "baaaaaaas" as I called them. Harmless! Not really, as one day in the dime store with Mom, I fixated on a flag I wanted and screamed so loud that the cranky, old clerk told us to leave the store. My mom was frustrated with me and mad at the clerk.

When I was five, Dad took me to a place called Happy Jacks. He wanted me to have a father-son experience. Dad wasn't the outdoor type, being more comfortable in a library or bookstore. Happy Jacks was a fishing pool stocked with fish so that anyone could land a fish. I saw a big fish and announced that I was going to catch it. Much to Dad's surprise, in a few minutes, I reeled it in. That evening we ate my fish. Guess who cleaned it!

In the summer of 1984, Pasadena hosted the Summer Olympics. My dad was given tickets to attend various events as he had contributed to the support of the games. We were sitting close to the action. We watched the track and field and the gymnastics competitions. I saw Mary Lou Retton perform. She was the first gymnast of her age to win a gold medal. I became hopelessly in love.

2

Developments

M Y MEMORIES of my early childhood are warm and happy, and yet I wasn't developing normally. I had been slow to talk and I had been held back in preschool while my peers graduated ahead of me. This was to become a familiar pattern.

My parents were concerned and met with a psychologist. A battery of tests were conducted but no precise diagnosis was forthcoming. I was labeled "developmentally delayed" because I was too young to be tested for a specific condition. Emotionally, I exhibited behaviors that alarmed one psychiatrist, who told my parents that by the time I entered my teens, I would have to be put into a mental institution.

Fortunately for me, that doctor was wrong. Right away, I was put into several tutoring classes where I received one-on-one help. The subject matter wasn't as important as the fact that I was getting individual attention, which helped me to focus and learn without distraction. In crowded settings, I tend to become anxious and unable to concentrate. My mom spent many days driving me to all my appointments. At home, she read to me and did a variety of activities to reinforce my learning. I did learn, but only by repetition and in a structured setting. Most of my public school education would be spent in special education classes.

At this time we were living in Pasadena, California. I was attending Bethany Christian Nursery School. I had a special teacher who told me that Jesus loved me. She explained how I could put my trust in Jesus and become a Christian. I did accept Jesus' love and have never regretted that decision. Of course, I didn't fully understand all the mystery connected with my decision. But, as I have grown, I have been able to see the difference Jesus has made in my life. Without him, I would have become a very different person. I am very thankful for that teacher.

One of my favorite tutors was Mrs. Pat. I met with her in her home where we practiced reading and sequencing. Afterwards, I got to play with her son, Matt. One time, Matt was playing with a toy that I wanted. When I asked him if I could have it, he refused. I was stumped until I thought to say, "God says, 'Share!'" And you know what? Matt did!

I thank God for my family. My parents and big sister have been supportive and encouraging. Being Christians has been a stabilizing influence for all of us. Without God's strength and help, I don't know where I would be today.

3

Mixed Blessings

A FTER NURSERY school, I was enrolled in the public grade school in Pasadena. I was put in the special ed class. I couldn't see anything "special" about it. I was isolated from the regular students and stuck in a basement room that used to be a storage room, which was located next to the school's kitchen. I had to be in this class because I was diagnosed as "emotionally disturbed." Who wouldn't be disturbed in a setting like that! My class was smaller than the regular classes and my teacher was supposed to give individual attention to each student. Usually, the misbehaving kids got her attention. My mom told me that when she approached my school building, she could hear my teacher yelling at the class. It was time to consider a family move as the California schools had a bad reputation and my personal experience was not good.

When I turned nine, Dad announced that we were moving to Marin County in northern California. I was excited to leave Pasadena. My family and I and my various pets headed north in two cars. At that time we had a dog, Marsh, who we had acquired in Nebraska. I had found and adopted a mouse, a toad, and a salamander. No way could I leave my pets behind. We moved into our new house, which was located on Vineyard Road, with open space and a creek running along the border of our property.

It was a place for a young boy to love. We had a variety of wildlife living in plain view. Deer with twins and triplets roamed the back woods. Possums, raccoons, skunks, and rats shared our land. Gophers were entrenched in our back yard and remained so for the eight years we lived in that house. My mom tried all sorts of disgusting ways to get rid of the gophers to no avail.

Our property had been an orchard of fruit and nut trees. We had Gravenstine apples, plums, figs, Bing cherries, and two walnut trees. Before we put up a fence, the deer would enter the yard and sit on mom's mulch pile and eat it! When the harvest of fruit and nuts overwhelmed us, we emptied buckets of the same over the back fence. Once, I forgot to tip my bucket and ended up literally hung over the fence till Mom yelled at me to let go the bucket. I hated those chores!

Unlike most of my friends, I had a dad who was also my pastor. Being a pastor's kid had its perks. Church folks always asked Dad how I was doing. I know that many people prayed for me and for my family. Being a pastor can be a hard calling, but many folks in the church knew of our family's challenges and supported us with their prayers.

When I was twelve years old, my dad baptized me. The baptism was done California style in a church member's pool! In Pasadena, we had our own pool and had loud youth group parties for my sister and her friends. I didn't learn to swim, but managed to ride my bike into the shallow end. Mom made me dry off my bike right away.

4

Added Challenges

I N MARIN, I continued my schooling in special ed classes because I needed an environment with few distractions but with emotional stability. Neither need was met in my new school. Since I was quiet in class, I was viewed as an asset. If I was an "asset," what did that make the other students? Many of these kids came from broken homes or dysfunctional families. Few of my classmates had positive role models. My parents and two or three other parents were the only ones who attended teacher conferences or open house events. This was discouraging for my folks and an isolating experience for my mom.

I had trouble making friends at school. Since I was slow to understand games and was shy, I spent most of the recesses alone. If I caught the attention of other kids, it usually took the form of them teasing me. I didn't know how to handle this and so I became angry. Mom would try to console me by telling me that kids who bully have their own problems. Their bullying behavior said more about them than it did about me.

Dad would also tell me that someday this bullying would stop. Dad was always very encouraging. He accepted and loved me. I realize that he was showing me what God thinks of me. There were times when I needed correction and Dad would give it. Did I appreciate Dad's correction? No! But I knew that Dad was correcting me out of his love for me.

I continued to have a hard time relating to kids my own age. Dad confronted me with the need to understand my angry emotions. He told me that getting angry doesn't solve anything. You just have to get to a place where you are no longer ruled by your emotions. Your bullies are not worth your holding on to your anger. They would have forgotten what they had done and you would still be stewing. This was sound advice but hard to put into practice. I understand that my frustrations feed my anger. I am making some progress in controlling or diverting my negative feelings into more constructive channels.

When I was sixteen years old, Dad taught me how to lift weights. He made me promise that I would never use steroids to build big muscles. He taught me to start gradually and not expect a sudden increase in strength. "It's like in life, David, you have to acquire new skills step by step. You can't suddenly become a genius, just like you can't suddenly lift 100 pounds." I have continued to weight train and can bench-press a considerable weight. My former bullies wouldn't recognize me now! Perseverance and keeping one's focus on the important goals is the way to go! I would still love to encounter some of my former bullies and show off my muscles!

There were several happy rewards during my junior high years in Marin. I was mainstreamed into several regular classes. That was a welcome change as I had new teachers and new classmates. I especially enjoyed art projects. I made a mobile that I entered into the Marin County Art Show and won an honorable mention. In English class, I wrote a story entitled "A Day in the Life of a Dog," for which I won an award. I also won a Bronze Key for doing so well in school. I became an honor roll member! I never imagined that I would become one of fifteen students to achieve this honor. My parents were so happy that I had been able to go beyond my earlier limitations.

5

The Family Man

I WAS lucky to have a loving and fun dad. I have many happy memories of my life with him. I hope that I will be able to model my life after his. My dad wasn't perfect, but he was perfect for me and my family. He modeled genuine Christian faith. And he created a place in my heart that will never be filled by anyone else.

Dad always made time for me and my family. We were his priority. When church people wanted to get together with Dad, he told them that he would have to check with his family first before making a commitment. When he interviewed for a new church job, he always stated that his family came first before the church and that the church was hiring him but not his family. Small churches tend to assume that hiring a pastor means that the wife will play a dual role in the church's activities.

My mom was much relieved to have their expectations put into proper perspective. She was not raised in a church and didn't hold to other people's expectations. Once, someone asked my mom if she would play the organ for the church service. Mom replied that she didn't play the organ or the piano but she could whistle! They never took her up on her offer. Her job was to be a good wife and mother.

Although my dad was very bright, he was able to be fun and even silly. He would refer to each of us by reversing the letters of our names. I became "Divad Yarb" Libby was "Ybbil Yarb," Mom was "Ronaele Yarb," and Dad was "Nhoj Yarb"! Years later, Libby has a daughter named "Gabi"— Ybbil and Gabi! Perfect!

Since Dad's initials were JSB, Mom referred to Dad as "Johann Sebastian Bray." Dad had a full beard and mustache most of his adult life. So when he and Mom were in Zaire for a pastors' conference, Dad was cast as Dr. Stanley Livingston for the skit night.

Mom managed most of the chores at home but felt that everyone should help out. So Dad came up with the idea of family workday alternating with family frolic day. This functioned fairly well, but it seemed that we did more frolicking than actual work.

6

Dad as a Pastor

AS SENIOR pastor, Dad viewed his staff as a team. Once a week, he met with the staff as a group and individually with each staff member. He was always willing to give each person the benefit of the doubt even if they goofed up. He would discuss ideas with folks who would then own them as their own. Dad didn't seek credit. He just wanted the job done correctly. Some of Dad's models were David Hubbard, John Stott, and Abraham Lincoln.

Dad was a Democrat. Invariably, when national elections were being held, Dad would be living in a Republican state. During his Florida State teaching years, Dad joined the ACLU. Back then the ACLU supported causes that helped the disadvantaged, not the disgruntled folks of later decades. Dad enjoyed local politics and helped the poor folk who always seem to live on the wrong side of the tracks. In Tallahassee, those folks lived in an area that routinely flooded.

Dad was a practical guy. "Just give me the facts, Max." When he was pastor in Pasadena, he was confronted with the need to remove several small apartments owned by the church so that a parking lot could be constructed. The city officials wanted the apartments saved for low-income families. After hassling with city officials, the buildings were removed without city permission. What could the city do? Now the congregation members could park off street and the neighbors were happy.

Dad didn't get bogged down in the details. He figured if a thing was worth doing well, then it was worth doing poorly, especially in order to get church folk to volunteer. If he could do something well, then someone else could also do it. He delegated assignments and didn't run the church as if it were a one-man show.

If there was a dispute between church members, Dad would figure out a way to solve the issue. For example, two farmers in Kansas had been feuding for years. So Dad invited each farmer to the church office, not mentioning that both would arrive at the same time. He proceeded to lock the two men into his office and told them that they could come out only after they had worked out their differences!

Dad didn't suffer from overconfidence. The first day on the job as pastor, he stood at the door of the church and wondered how he had arrived at that place. He had spent the past decade as a university professor. He was familiar with the secular world. How would he fare in a religious environment? Not only did Dad survive but he became an effective spiritual leader as pastor of three Covenant churches followed by the deanship at North Park Seminary.

7

Dad as a Teacher

DAD WAS always popular with his students but an embarrassment to the administration. At the end of Dad's fourth year teaching at Wayne State College, the president of the college fired him. However, the students voted Dad the most popular teacher for that year. The president was forced to reinstate Dad. At that point, Dad shook the dust off his feet and resigned! I forgot to mention that Dad was president of the faculty senate at the time and had raised issues that forced the president, a former military man, to make changes that he didn't want to make.

Dad was a master teacher who had a gift for being able to study complex concepts and express them in terms that the average person could understand. He would present the various philosophies, their strengths, and weaknesses. Then he would compare them to his own Christian beliefs and allow the students to draw their own conclusions. On the matter of millennialism, Dad would say that he was a "panmillennialist—Everything would pan out in the end."

One student, John, had a hunger for knowledge, which Dad fed. Weekly the two Johns would meet in Dad's office to discuss philosophy. Each week Dad would give the student a book to take home and read. After several months, the student was quite confused and just wanted an explanation of what Dad believed concerning the nature of God. Afterwards, the student wanted to know how to become a believer. Dad never forced his beliefs onto other people.

Dad was widely read and had an extensive library including Western philosophy and church history. He was able to translate several languages and had studied abroad in France and Lake Geneva doing research for his doctorate, entitled "Beza's Interpretation of Calvin's Doctrine of Predestination."

Dad's desk was never clean. In fact, his filing system consisted of piles of papers. Somehow, he managed to locate whatever he was looking for in all the mess. He used to say that a clean desk is a sign of an empty mind. His mind was never idle. He enjoyed a wide range of interests and never tired of exercising his brain.

Dad liked to keep busy and challenge his mind. While teaching and later pastoring, he spoke at many InterVarsity Christian Fellowship camps. Once, on very short notice, he replaced a famous speaker who suddenly became ill. Dad spent the entire camp time hunched over a very inadequate desk, preparing his talks. Dad's talks were more like rapid-fire lectures. Students had a hard time keeping up with his lectures and Scripture references. His bibliographies were massive. One student quipped that John Bray had killed more trees than any other professor he knew!

Dad changed careers many times during his life. When we moved to Chicago, Dad became dean of North Park Seminary and entered administrative work. He was a gifted administrator and referred to himself as a change agent. Some of the faculty would soon learn that he would change their lives, and not to their liking.

While Dad was dean, he taught classes at North Park University. In one class, he explained the concept of "the essence of being" in the following way. He drew a simple sketch of our Beagle, Katie, on the board. He said, "This is a dog, right? If I erase her tail, she is still a dog. If I continue to erase her legs, is she still a dog?" The students got the point. I Googled "essence of being" and was confronted with a five-chapter examination of the subject that was totally incomprehensible to me. Thank God for Dad's ability to simplify!

I admire my dad because he worked so hard. He was the only one in his family to complete college. He worked his way through school, never receiving support from his family. He applied for grants and scholarships and persevered when he was turned down by all but the last grantor. Dad changed careers several times and had to reenter the teaching profession after an absence of almost twenty years. He remained current by spending many hours in bookstores, researching the latest scholarship in his field of study.

8

Midwest Years

WE WERE moving again. I was in my junior year and ready for a change. I had lived most of my life in California and would now move to the Midwest. Dad had been offered the job of dean at North Park Seminary located in Chicago. My parents were from the Midwest and remembered long, cold, gray winters. We would be living in the "windy city." Our thin California clothes would not protect us from the freezing winds off Lake Michigan. Burlington Coat Factory came to the rescue, where we each bought a down jacket.

We were now somewhat prepared to meet the elements. Our poor Beagle detested the cold, wet stuff covering the ground. Our first winter, we experienced a tremendous snowstorm. Where was our confused dog going to do her business? We eased her confusion by shoveling a path and "poop" area in the backyard. Katie spent little time relieving herself before she made a mad dash back into the warm house. I, however, marveled at the mounds of snow and the huge icicles that hung from our roof. I had other weather adventures to get used to—thunder! Until recent years, you never heard thunder in California.

Our new home was located in Skokie, where I attended Niles North High School. I elected to enroll as a junior so that I could make up the courses I hadn't had in California. I also participated in several after-school, part-time jobs to gain work experience. I especially enjoyed working at the North Park Physical Plant. I learned to do maintenance work in the student dorms. Leroy was my coach and friend. He noticed my skinny body and decided to do something about it. He helped me weight train during our breaks. He even devised a rope belt when my pants started to fall off! It is hard for me to believe that I was so thin back then. Leroy was a wonderful friend and great Christian.

After my high school graduation, Dad and I took a trip to Las Vegas to celebrate my twenty-first birthday. We played many games of chance and won at video poker, slots, and craps. I wonder who first called that game "craps." It must have been a loser. I won so much money that I was able to pay half of my college tuition. In the Imperial Palace, I saw a car that had been made for Adolph Hitler. It was autographed by the Jews who had been forced to make it. I also saw a car that was built for Al Capone. There were other cars that had belonged to past presidents of the United States. Aside from the casinos, eating out was amazing and inexpensive.

My dad was a great model of how to deal with negative emotions. He had a hot temper, but I never saw him angry or out of control. He had grown up with a dad who was an alcoholic. Dad was gentle. I find it easy to imagine Christ being strong and masculine as well as loving and gentle because of the example of my dad.

When high school was over, I applied to go to Covenant Bible College, which was an affiliate of the Covenant denomination. I was accepted and attended their one-year program. I wasn't sure I could handle college studies, but Dad encouraged me to try. The school was in Strathmore, Alberta, Canada. It was my first year living away from my family. I adjusted as well as could be expected as I missed my family, especially my dad. If I thought Chicago was cold, Alberta exceeded my expectations! But because of the northern location, I saw the northern lights and clear, star-filled skies. I made good friends among the Christian students.

CBC was a huge challenge for me. I struggled academically but still benefited from being away from home and living in a Christian community. While my grades were quite low, I persevered and survived my year of studies and living away from home. Dad contributed money for weight training equipment, and I was allowed to paint a mural on one wall of the weight room. I made some great friends and had the experience of living in a guys' dorm. I even had my ear pierced—to the surprise of my dad and the horror of my mom! CBC has since closed, but it provided a Christian environment for young adults to transition from high school into adult life.

9

On My Own?

I RETURNED to Chicago after graduation and lived at home with my parents. I was at loose ends and had no plan for my future. I couldn't handle a job and was bored at home. I slumped into a pattern of watching TV late at night. The programs were less than inspiring and more often sexually provocative. I was sinking fast into moral brain rot. Dad and I knew that I needed a change.

What was I going to do now that I was graduated from college? I couldn't handle further academic education and I wasn't able to continue working at the Physical Plant. Dad knew that I was getting "itchy feet," wanting to leave home and be with other guys my age. At the same time, he knew that, because of my disabilities, I was not ready for complete independence.

While we were still living in California, Dad had been investigating possibilities. He was always looking out for what was best for me. Dad was a Covenant pastor and had connections within the denomination. He had contacted the folks at an inner-city Christian community called Jesus People USA. He knew about this place, as it was an official church of the Evangelical Covenant denomination. JPUSA had its beginning in the Jesus movement and was unique among the Covenant congregations. He was impressed with what he discovered and thought it might be perfect for me someday.

Remembering his previous investigation into this community, Dad contacted them and asked if I could visit on a trial basis. It was agreed that I would live at JPUSA for a two-week period to see if I would like it. After those two weeks, I felt confident that JPUSA was where God wanted me to be.

I remember when I moved in; Mom was very emotional. She had seen the room that I would be sharing with three other guys and she was upset. She had raised me in middle-class suburbia. Now, her son would be living in tight quarters in a room the size of an average walk-in closet. "Eleanor, my dad said in a consoling voice, 'At least he's not moving to China!'" Mom glared at him. He didn't get it that her middle-class sensibilities were being severely challenged.

Except for my decision to accept Christ as my personal Savior, moving to JPUSA was the best thing that ever happened to me. I now have more Christian friends than I can count. When I experience depression or have any kind of need, I can seek out almost anyone here. I live independently but my meals are provided. Each week I am visited by a student nurse from Loyola. I enjoy weekly maid service. How many people do you know who are on SSI and have a maid? I also have a clear view of Lake Michigan from my window!

10

JPUSA

Jesus People USA is a community of Christian singles and families. A variety of ministries serve the needs of the homeless and abused in the Uptown area of Chicago. The community occupies a ten-story building. Formerly a neighborhood of drug dealers and pimps, the area is slowly being changed by the influx of yuppies with money. It will be years before this area is fully transformed.

At JPUSA the single brothers and single sisters live on separate floors. Families are interspersed on all floors except the top floors, which are home to senior folks. When the building was first acquired, there were indigents living in squalid conditions. In order to buy the site from the city of Chicago, JPUSA had to agree to support and operate a retirement community for senior citizens. Small apartments are provided along with meals, maid service, activities and outings, and simple medical help.

Many young people are attracted to JPUSA. Word of mouth or attendance at the annual Cornerstone Music Festival have drawn new folks to the ministry. Several businesses owned and operated by JPUSA folks support the community. Guys new to JPUSA are assigned to the dish crew. The gals provide waitressing and maid service for the seniors. When I first visited JPUSA, I wasn't sure that I wanted to live there. So, I was allowed to stay for a trial visit of two weeks. After my visit, I decided to commit for one year, knowing that I would be faced with many challenges and hard adjustments.

When I moved to JPUSA I started working in the kitchen washing dishes and scrubbing floors. As the saying goes, "If you can handle the dish crew, you can handle anything." The goal here at the House is to learn to be a servant—what better way than washing someone else's dirty dishes! Dad visited me occasionally to see how I was surviving. I managed to work on the dish crew for six-and-a-half months. I sure had many opportunities to learn servanthood!

Because JPUSA housed several hundred individuals, many of whom had come out of abusive families or who had abused drugs, strict rules and swift discipline had to be maintained. I had a hard adjustment dealing with some of these rules. Looking back, I can understand why many of the rules were required. Most of the rules were made to help those people who were not Christians or were young in their walk with God.

Many of the people here have made a 180-degree turn in the direction of their lives. Some folks were deeply involved in drugs, alcohol, sex, and everything else that comes with that kind of lifestyle. These folks are now living for Jesus and following his lead. Temptations are many, but the rules help these people to resist. Many folks think that they are "called" to ministry at JPUSA. But, to quote a movie that JPUSA made a few years ago, "Many are called but few can stand it!"

About this time, Dad investigated the possibility for me to receive SSI benefits. He wanted to make sure that I would have a secure future. It had been established that I would be unable to work to support myself as I had been diagnosed as having a mental illness. After filling out many forms and submitting them to the local Social Security office, we waited for news of my acceptance. When we learned that my application had been accepted, I was relieved. I could continue to live at JPUSA.

I was officially classified as "disabled." I receive a monthly check that pays for my room and board and other expenses. Peace and quiet at last. I had moved off the sixth floor where I had shared a small room with three other guys. Our room had its own bathroom, which we had to share with other guys across the hall. Now, I had my own room and private bath. I could lock my door and know that my things were safe. I could take a nap or go to bed early if I needed extra sleep. I am grateful for my situation here.

11

Life in the House

WHEN I moved to JPUSA, Dad continued to spend time with me. He called often and asked how I was doing. If he sensed that I was depressed—a common emotion for folks new to JPUSA—he would invite me out to eat and spend time talking.

We would discuss the things I was experiencing, and Dad would calmly reassure me that things would work out. We would pray together and ask for God's help. My dad's reliance on prayer has always impressed me. Now I have become committed to praying about everything. I am thankful for my dad because he remained beside me, encouraging and comforting me. Because he continued to show support for me, my adventure in community living has been a huge success. God has used this community to help me grow spiritually, emotionally, and socially.

I have been employed at the same job for almost ten years. I work at Belly Acres, a tee shirt design company that is owned and operated by JPUSA. My job was to pull shirts off the drying racks. Although my job assignment has changed, I am still responsible to my boss, Darren. He is understanding of my limitations. He encourages me to do my very best but doesn't expect more of me than I am able to give.

I know that I have surpassed my dad's expectations for me in the years I have lived at JPUSA. I have even surprised myself. I have become more independent as a person and more reliant upon God. One of the areas of growth has been in my ability to manage my emotions. I have a problem dealing appropriately with anger. At JPUSA, I am learning to control my negative feelings and show the other person some understanding. Being "right" isn't as important as being kind. The Bible has helped me to focus on the important issues. I listen to the Bible on CD and have memorized many verses.

12

The Fest

ONE OF the biggest events that JPUSA hosts is a Christian music extravaganza called Cornerstone Festival. It takes place outside a farming village south of Peoria in the heartland of Illinois. Each year, most of the JPUSA folks gather at Bushnell to organize and set up stages and tents to welcome the hundreds of music lovers for a weekend of music saturation, lectures, and seminars. The Bushnell community welcomes this annual event because security is tight and no problems have occurred with such large gatherings.

JPUSA owns several acres of farmland where the Fest is held. Campsites are available close to the performing tents or further away in the woods. While the Fest is primarily a venue for Christian contemporary music, other activities are provided. Creation Station is set up for children to engage in craft and art projects. Recreational activities are available, including boating and swimming in a nearby lake.

My first summer at the Fest, I shared a tent with my good friend Tom. We arrived a few days early to help with the setup. Huge tents were put up for the concerts and smaller tents for the seminars. Our own tent was close to one of the concert tents.

One night we experienced a torrential rainstorm! Flashing lightening, roaring thunder, and howling wind: this was my introduction to Midwest weather. I could see our tent's roof caving in due to the weight of the rain. This was scary stuff! I had grown up in southern California and had never experienced such a storm.

Tom could see that I was rattled. He told me that we would be ok. We prayed and I eventually fell asleep. We awoke next morning to soggy sleeping bags and a sea of mud outside. I soon learned that rain was an annual event for the Fest!

13

Dad

MY DAD was a very private man concerning his feelings. He didn't want anyone to worry about his problems. As he grew up, he had learned to keep his feelings to himself. His dad was an abusive alcoholic. Dad grew up in a tough environment inside the home and in the neighborhood. Showing one's feelings in the slums of Detroit would suggest weakness and invite trouble. A person had to be tough to survive.

On his last night, Dad and I went out to eat but Dad wasn't his usual jovial self. I could sense that something was bothering him. When I asked him if anything was wrong, he told me not to worry. "It's small potatoes." That was his way of telling me that he didn't want me to worry about him. I really wished that he had opened up.

When we got home, he went off to his study where he could be alone. I stood by his study door but didn't enter the room. He was sitting with his face in his hands and his head bowed in prayer. "Oh God, my body is falling apart and I don't know what I am going to do."

The next day was November 28, the day that he died. I've often thought how glad I am that our last words together were words of love. I don't have to wish that I had not said something hurtful or that I hadn't let him know how much I loved him. We must be careful about what we say to loved ones, as that may be the last thing they hear from us.

When we were cleaning out Dad's university office, we discovered several books dealing with parenting children with disabilities. Dad was a voracious reader and learned much from reading books. I know that my dad loved me and did his best to be supportive, affectionate, and challenging. If he had not challenged me, I probably would have stopped trying a long time ago. Dad never looked down on me for being disabled. He treated me with respect. I was his son and he let me know that he was proud of me.

14

After My Dad Was Gone

SEVERAL DAYS after my Dad's memorial service, the finality of his death hit me. My dad was gone. I would never see him again and never be comforted by him. In the past I could always call up my dad and he would have just the right things to say—a joke that would lift my spirits or a simple prayer that would bring comfort. Now, all contact was cut off. I was alone. Even though I had my family and many friends at JPUSA, my life would never be the same. I was experiencing a profound loss and nothing brought comfort. Bedtimes were the worst. Many nights I cried myself to sleep.

The thought of Dad being in heaven brought no comfort. I imagined him floating around in the who-knows-where, wearing wings, singing songs, and playing a harp. No one has ever come back from heaven, so my ideas of it were pretty sketchy, even ridiculous. I couldn't imagine Dad playing a harp for eternity. Floating in the sky seemed impossible and meaningless.

When the shock wore off, I became extremely angry at God for taking Dad away from me. Why did Dad have to leave now? Why did God want Dad in heaven? I found no comfort in well-meaning comments of friends. I missed Dad and wanted him back in my life. And I was angry at my dad for leaving me.

One night, I had a dream in which I saw my dad. I was mystified and a little frightened. I soon realized that Dad was trying to comfort me! In my dream, Dad appeared in my room and greeted me. He spoke: "Hi David. Look at me! I now have real hair. Touch it, even pull it!" I touched it, and sure enough, it was real! Instead of being bald and wearing a hairpiece, Dad now had a full head of brown hair.

"My skin is no longer cancer-prone. Instead, it is as pure as new skin! I have no more slipped disks in my back. It is fine and strong." Dad was moving and rebounding around my room in a way that he had not been able to move for many years. No longer was my dad suffering with weight problems. "Wow!" I exclaimed enthusiastically. "You are looking so good, Dad!"

"The changes you see in me are 'heavenly,'" Dad chuckled. "Imagine living in a place where everyone is in harmony with everyone else. There are no more fights or arguments or bad feelings. No more bullies, Dave! The biggest joy for me is living in the presence of Jesus."

"I want to come and be with you in heaven, Daddy!"

He smiled at me and said, "Someday we will be together again, but it is not your time. God has made you and is in the process of preparing you to do special things for him. I will see you here someday, David."

My dream ended. I had so many questions to ask Dad. I wanted him to remain with me, but I was somehow comforted by his brief presence. Seeing him enjoying his glorified body had been a wonderful experience. I was filled with joy knowing that he was now living in the presence of Jesus and was no longer burdened by physical problems and health issues. He had died of complications due to diabetes and congestive heart failure. Thank God, my dad was now free from all earthly burdens.

A feeling of hope now softened my grieving heart. I had "seen" my dad and knew that he was in a better place. I knew where my dad had gone and that he was enjoying his new life. I was happy for him. Now I could begin to have closure regarding his death. The life we live on Earth is but a preparation for our life in eternity. Earthly life is a dress rehearsal for the real life to come. Christian apologist C. S. Lewis referred to our life on Earth as being in the "shadow-lands." My dad was now out of the shadows and basking in the true light!

I was greatly comforted by my dream. My dad was in a real heaven and with a real God. This assurance can be available to anyone who loses a loved one if that loved one had a relationship with our heavenly Father. The Bible says in Romans 8:28 that "in everything God works for good with those who love him, who are called according to his purpose."

Buddies

Kansas

Libby and "Dadid"

Dress-ups

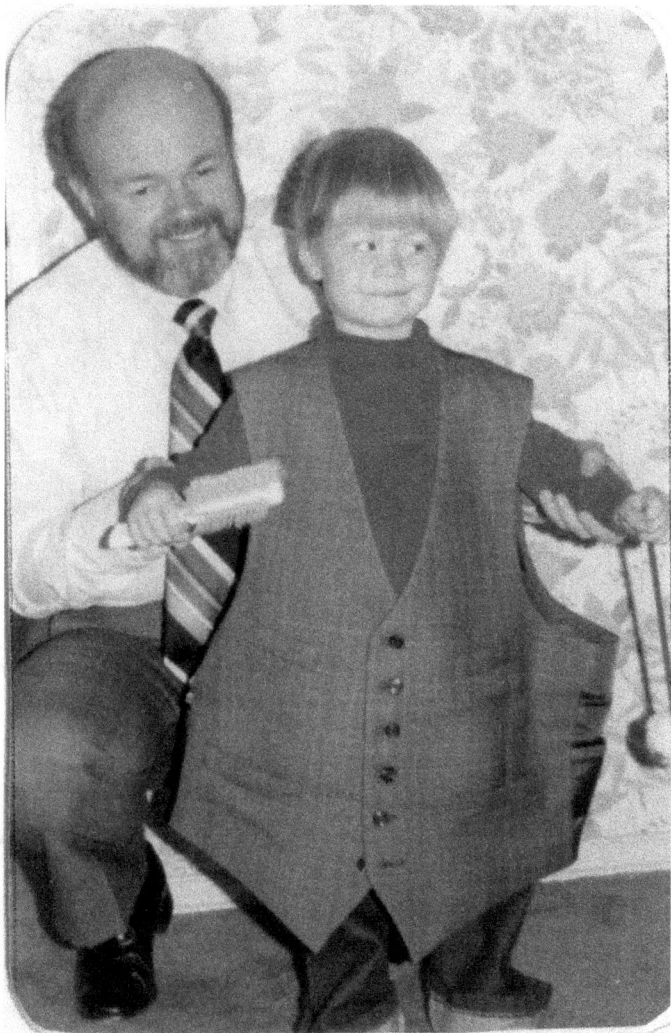

Off to work

David and Sean

LA Olympics

Charlie Chaplin

Chicago

Libby and Joe's Wedding

Last Family Christmas Together

Our Nutty Family

Trekkie

David Bray and John Bray in one creature
12/15/9

Joined at the hip

Angels

15

Dreams

ONE OF the ways that God comforts me is through my dreams. God tells me that he is proud of me and reminds me that I am never alone. When I am in my room, God or Dad come to me and I feel surrounded by their love. Some of my friends are bitter over the death of one of their parents. Thankfully, I feel no bitterness. I know that Dad is in a place where he no longer suffers and yet he is still alive. Sickness is no longer a reality for him. Since my dad's death, my relationship with my heavenly Father has grown and flourished.

When Dad died, many brothers and sisters at JPUSA spent time with me, praying for and encouraging me. We even joked together, which helped to put things in perspective. I can't count the number of friends I have here at JPUSA. This family of believers is strong and God has used them greatly in my life. One such friend is Tom, who has been helping me write this book.

I have had many more dreams of my dad. In one dream, Dad said that he wished that death was not a part of life because he didn't want to leave me behind. He tried to comfort me by reminding me that God has promised us that he will never leave us. "God will be with you all the time, in good times and in bad times. David, you are in a place where people love you. Don't lose sight of that. Keep your focus on God and remember the words of the song, 'Turn your eyes upon Jesus, Look full in his wonderful face, And the things of Earth will grow strangely dim, In the light of his glory and grace.'"

The assurance that God will never abandon me gives me courage to face each new day and each new challenge. It is comforting to realize that God can do great things through our dreams. I want to be at peace with what God allows to happen. It is neat that he used my dad while he was alive and has continued to use him through my dreams.

Amazingly, I had had dreams that warned me that my dad might die. These dreams began a whole year before his death. In the dreams, I would see my dad collapse and die. I guess I was processing the fact that Dad was sick, having had congestive heart failure in Marin and again in Chicago. I also realized that Dad wasn't as energetic as before. When I shared my dreams with Dad, he assured me that he was not going to die for a long time and that I shouldn't worry about it. In hindsight, it gave me no satisfaction knowing that I had been right.

Then it happened. One morning Dad was on his way to teach his class at North Park University. As he walked across campus, he experienced a massive heart attack. He was rushed to the hospital but it was too late to save him. I know now that my dreams were God's way of preparing me for the horrendous ordeal of losing my father. After several years of grieving, I can be thankful that Dad is no longer suffering. I am also thankful that he didn't linger, enduring a slow decline. I would be able to remember him as I had always known him. But I will always miss our times together.

16

Encouragement

ILIVE in a Christian community, Jesus People USA, which is located in Uptown Chicago. I have many friends who care for me. If I have a problem and need someone to talk to, I have countless friends who lovingly give me the time to listen to me. I often knock on their door, share my problems, and then we pray together.

When Jesus was on Earth, he had experiences such as ours. He suffered loses as well. His best friend, Lazarus, died. This loss caused Jesus to weep. On the cross, Jesus felt totally alone while he suffered his crucifixion. How much more, then, could Jesus identify with my losses. Jesus experienced all of the emotions we experience. Was Jesus ever angry? Yes! Knowing that he got angry helps me to deal with my anger. It comforts me knowing that I am not alone in my struggles. God is always with me, holding me in his awesome, all-powerful hands. Whenever I feel overwhelmed by my problems, I can turn to him and he will help me.

I know that going through challenging experiences can make us stronger. The Bible says in Philippians 4:13, "I can do all things in him who strengthens me." The ability to master the situation doesn't have to be mine alone. God will help me. Sometimes he helps through brothers and sisters in the faith. Other times he helps us directly through reminders of Scripture. God has used my experiences to help other folks who are grieving.

We have been promised in the Bible that God will never allow us to go through anything that is bigger than we can handle. He helps us through his Holy Spirit. We need to hold on to the promises that God has given to us. Even in the "terrible, horrible, very bad days," God is bigger than our problems.

17

Prayer

SOMETIMES PEOPLE become impatient with me because I am still grieving my dad's death. They tell me to just get over it. This is easy for them to say because they haven't lost their confidant, counselor, friend, and father in one blow. Thankfully, many other people have been praying for me and my family.

Prayer is a powerful gift. It is our way of talking with God. As a result of seeing the tremendous good that prayer can accomplish and because of the strength that I received through prayer support, I have become a real prayer warrior. I have become a ready friend for other folks who need prayer. I love helping in this way. Dad was pleased that I had learned the value of prayer. The Bible reminds us that in our weakness, God is made strong. When I pray about a problem, it doesn't seem so heavy. A great deal of the weight has been shouldered by Christ himself.

I have also been given the gift of encouragement. My mom, my sister, and her husband all have this gift. It is a neat privilege to be able to help another person. Christ has come to me in my dreams, reminding me that in every situation, he is with me.

The promises of God are powerful. All through the Bible there are treasures to be found that remind us of our special relationship with God. We are his adopted children and members in his family of faith. We have been made in his image and he desires to have a relationship with us. God has promised in Hebrews 13:5, "I will never fail you nor forsake you." He says in Deuteronomy 31:6, "Be strong and of good courage, do not fear or be in dread of them: for it is the Lord your God who goes with you; he will not fail you or forsake you."

18

From B Team to A Team

IREMEMBER asking God to tell me what Dad was thinking when he died. God assured me that Dad was thinking of his family. When I said goodbye to Dad as his body lay in the hospital, I thought that would be the last time that I would talk to him. But that evening I had a dream in which Dad told me that I was to take care of my mom and sister. My mom and I didn't have the close relationship that Dad and I had enjoyed. Because I felt so close to Dad, I didn't want to include Mom.

Now that Dad was gone, my mom was my only parent. How was I going to share my deep feelings with her? Mom told me that sons typically favor their dads. This didn't erase my guilt for having pushed my mom away. My JPUSA friend Tom prayed daily with me that God would give me love for my mom. I didn't want to hate her or wish that she had died instead of my dad. But my anger was overtaking my thoughts and making it impossible to be comforted by her.

Thankfully, my mom seemed to understand my conflicting feelings and gave me space and time to sort things out. When I began to trust Mom with my grief, she became my best friend. As she expressed her new role, she had been moved from her son's B team to her son's A team. Humor expressed exactly how I felt.

Six months after Dad's passing, Mom told me that she had breast cancer. I was really frightened. "God, my dad is gone and now you are going to take my mom too? This isn't fair." However, Mom survived surgery and has been free of cancer for nine years. Her cancer had been caught at a very early stage. She didn't have to have chemo or radiation. Mom became my hero.

Several years later, I realized that something was wrong with my vision. I had been wearing glasses since elementary school. After a routine exam with my eye doctor, I was referred to a specialist. It was discovered that I had a rare eye condition called Keratoconus. Instead of my corneas having a symmetrical curved surface, they were changing shape, throwing my focus off to the degree that I thought that I was going blind. The corneal "cones" had become progressively distorted.

Some people can manage using hard contacts. In my case, the corneas were changing shape so rapidly that the hard contacts kept popping off my eyes. The whole process was very frustrating, as neither Mom nor I had ever used contacts. Mom helped me to learn placement and removal techniques. What a disaster that was! I begged for surgery, hoping it would free me from so much frustration. Finally, I had my first transplant operation in 2006. Mom was there with me through the whole process. I stayed at her apartment for two weeks after surgery, learning to put drops in my eye. I had several kinds of drops that I had to use.

Soon I was back at JPUSA, grossing out my friends with my descriptions of my surgery. The hardier folk wanted to look at my eye to see if they could see the dozen or so stitches that held the donated cornea in pace. We learned that the cornea had come from a young man who had been in a fatal bike accident. It was a strange but wonderful feeling to have a part of someone helping me to see. Healing progressed slowly as the donor cornea was missing some peripheral tissue.

The doctor told us on a routine visit that light was slowing the healing process. If he could stitch my eye closed, healing would progress faster. He proceeded to stitch my eyelids shut in his office. That was the most painful experience I had yet endured. Mom and I both gritted our teeth. After one year, the second eye was operated on with great success. Healing took place quickly. I learned to use the various drops on my own. Soon the anti-rejection drops were no longer necessary. I now put one drop in each eye three times daily. I thank God for people who are willing to be donors. I am now able to see well without contacts.

My mom has become my best friend. She has helped me through some rough times.

19

My Mom

THIS STORY has focused almost entirely on my Dad. Now I would also like to share some details about my relationship with my mom. She has emerged from behind the "shadow" of my dad's presence and has become my new best friend. She has been understanding and gentle in her encouragement. We talk frequently by phone and get together once a week.

I look forward to our weekly times together. Mom is a great cook and always has something yummy for lunch. Everything she makes is from scratch. My favorite green vegetable is okra. Dad couldn't stand it! Mom's roast beef and juice bread are to die for! On Halloween, Mom bakes the pumpkin seeds and sends me back to JPUSA with a big jar of them.

Mom has taught me not to give up on myself because of my disabilities. She encourages me to keep trying new things. I have also learned to be brave because of her example. The death of Dad and Mom's diagnosis of breast cancer six months later allowed me to observe her emotional strength and her reliance upon God. The Bible says, "they who wait for the Lord shall renew their strength, they shall mount up with wings like eagles, they shall run and not be weary, they shall walk and not faint" (Isaiah 40:31).

In the years 2006-2007, I had surgery on my eyes to replace both corneas. Through it all, Mom was my companion and encourager. I hate to imagine going through all of that alone. Mom was God's provision of strength for me. She was by my side, praying for me.

My mom has a low tolerance for my homemade puns. If I tell you one that needs "improving," she tells me not to quit my day job. She recently reminded me of an incident when I was still a little guy. One day, we were in the kitchen and I wanted to get her attention. So I said, "Mom." She ignored me, so I repeated "Mom" several more times. Finally, she turned to me and told me to stop "moming" her. After some moments passed, I said, "Dad?"!!!

My mom has a high tolerance for the absurd. Let me explain. She let me bring home two "pets" we had found while on a hike in the Angeles Crest foothills: Sally and Toady-kee-hoadie. Housing them would be no problem. We had a fish aquarium. But feeding them would be a challenge, as Dad used to say. After reading up on toad and salamander diets, Mom came up with a ready and free solution. She had a worm farm in the back yard. Serious gardeners usually have such a thing tucked away at the back of their property. Worms would be the food of choice for Sally.

Toady presented a different challenge. Toads eat live, moving bait. Hmmmmmm. Mom hit upon the plan to stun flies, which she did by swatting them on the brick sidewalk with a fly swatter. Not wanting to entertain the neighbors too often, she kept a handy supply of stunned flies in a baggie in the refrigerator! It was quite a sight watching Sally gulp down a worm or seeing Toady leap up in the air after a fly! We kept Toady and Sally for several years and released them back into the wild when we moved to northern California.

Other pets followed. A mouse, Mousey, lived in a cage on the kitchen counter and munched on the edges of Mom's cook books. Mouse owners will agree that mice smell like popcorn, that is, their urine. Bleck! Speaking of popcorn, one Christmas Mom played a joke on Dad. We had a box of foam popcorn. Mom decided to have an impromptu snowstorm. She upended the box of foam over Dad's head! We thought it was hilarious, but he just sat there looking at us over his reading glasses.

Another time, Mom, knowing that Dad was going to drive to the video store, hid in the backseat of his car, crouching over the hump on the floor. Dad had a habit of talking to himself when he was alone. He slowly drove to the store in his own little world while Mom tried not to split a gut and burst out laughing. Just as Dad parked the car, Mom reached out and touched his shoulder. Dad gasped and turned around. He told Mom, *"Never do that again!"* She never did! Mom made my life fun. She was a good counterbalance to Dad's serious nature.

20

Libby

LIBBY IS my big sister. She is a redhead with an independent spirit. Even though she is much shorter and smaller than me, sometimes I can be intimidated by her. I wonder how I will manage when Mom is gone. Don't get me wrong. Libby is a great sister and will stick up for me to the death! She encourages me and challenges me to try new things and is amazed by my accomplishments.

Libby was my first babysitter. She would take me into her room and play dress up with me. I have classic photos of me dressed as a little girl, complete with pinkie rings and lipstick. I loved the attention and didn't know enough at that age to be embarrassed. In later years, I dressed up our dogs in similar fashion!

Libby also taped our playtime talks. She had a tape recorder and asked me to repeat lots of words. She would say, "David, say 'dog.'" Then I would repeat the word. Finally, I had had enough of her game: When she asked me to say a new word, I clammed up!

Libby liked to dress up for the various holidays. One Easter, she dressed up as the Easter bunny, complete with a ping pong ball for a nose. Our church celebrated Santa Lucia every year. Libby was selected to be the young woman who wore a wreath with candles on her head. According to tradition, she would go from room to room on the morning of Santa Lucia Day (December 13), waking up the children.

I had great times with Libby. When she went to college, I saw less of her. She always came home for the holidays. One summer Libby's photo was used on a brochure for Calvin College. She was quite attractive, with her auburn hair and blue eyes. Libby has been firm in her Christian faith while many of her high school friends have drifted away. She is proud of our family and proud of me. When she became engaged, she made Joe promise to take care of me if something happened to her.

Libby and Joe frequently tell me that they would love for me to move to California. I have considered moving but realize that I am best off living in Chicago near Mom. JPUSA is my home, and the people there are my Christian family. I have a big group of friends, my meals are provided, and I have my own room.

I am becoming more independent managing my money. I have a caseworker who gives me advice, and my mom also helps me with my finances. Chicago is easy to get around by public transportation, and O'Hare Airport is twenty minutes away. After Dad died, Libby and Joe called me twice a week to find out how I was doing. It was a great comfort to have them care for me. I thank God for my great sister.

21

Joe

LIBBY MARRIED an awesome man of God. In the beginning, I felt jealous when my sister was falling in love and spending time with Joe. Libby didn't spend as much time with me and I felt left out. When the time came for the wedding, I wasn't sure that I wanted to attend. I am very glad that I made the decision to go with my parents to California for the ceremony.

During the week of wedding preparations, Joe went out of his way to help me get to know him. And Libby and Joe had a surprise for me. It was a piece of paper with a signature on it. Reggie Jackson, the famous baseball player, had been eating in a local LA restaurant! Libby recognized him and rushed over and asked for his autograph! Libby has a knack for spotting famous movie actors and has begged several autographs for her "needy" bro in Chicago. I hope she didn't go so far as to say I was on my deathbed and their autograph was my dying wish!

The week of preparation was hectic. I was able to share the excitement that my sister felt. All my life I had wanted to wear a tux. The wedding was the most beautiful ceremony I have ever attended. I regret feeling jealous because Joe has proven to be a great husband for Libby and a very caring brother for me.

Joe was born in Billings, Montana, but never knew his biological parents. He was adopted and grew up in a Christian home with two siblings. When Joe met Libby, he was a graphic designer but felt called to ministry. Presently, he is the associate pastor at a church in Orange County, California. He leads worship and preaches when the senior pastor is away. He is an effective communicator and has a gentle spirit.

When my dad died, Joe stepped up and took Dad's place. Joe was very comforting and would pray with me about my problems. Sometimes I would hear demonic voices telling me that I had no worth and that I should kill myself. Joe assured me that I was worthy of God's love and that I should tell Satan to bug off. Joe seemed to sense when I was struggling and would give me a phone call.

Joe has been a big blessing in my life. He considers me his brother and respects me. I sense that he is awed by my accomplishments and doesn't look down on me. He loves my puns (some exceptions) and my rap music. I am a better man for knowing Joe.

22

Those Who Have Gone Before

THE OTHER night, I went to bed very tired and imme-
diately fell into a deep sleep. As I slept, Dad appeared
to me in a dream. He was not alone. I saw many family
members, including Dad's parents and my mother's mother.
Dad said, "We are here waiting for you, David. When it's
your time and God brings you home, we are going to have
a party!" At that moment they all clapped and exclaimed,
"We love you, David. Keep it up and we'll see you soon.
Continue to live for the Lord. Make that your priority."

It was great to know that my loved ones were thinking
of me, praying for me and looking forward to our meeting
in heaven. But it is sad when people who do not know Jesus
as their Savior die. There is no hope for them after death
and no assurance of reunion with past loved ones.

The wonderful thing for believers is that physical
death isn't our end but a new beginning. God has made this
promise to us: "I am with you always, to the close of the age"
(Matthew 28:20). It is wonderful to have such promises that
we can trust. Unlike commitments made by people, God's
promises are sure. God will never revoke his word.

23

Depression and Other Emotions

I HAVE struggled with many bouts of depression over the years. For one thing, I am still a single guy. All the women I like are either too young, too old, or already taken. I meet many gals who come to JPUSA to visit. As soon as I start feeling any sort of attraction toward them, they announce that they are leaving Chicago. Am I destined to be single for the rest of my life?

After my latest rejection I went to bed in a foul mood. I was angry and feeling sorry for myself. My bad mood increased and I blamed God for all my woes. Sometime in the night Dad began to comfort and encourage me. He told me not to lose heart. Life is full of disappointments. We all have desires that are not met. We have plans that never work out. But remember that God knows what is best for us, and he tries to steer us in the right direction.

At the time I wanted to debate with Dad. Great counsel is great but didn't make me feel any better. It has only been in hindsight that I have seen the wisdom of my dad's words. Several of the gals I had been attracted to turned out to be real jerks. One gal was even married when she was flirting with me! Another one already had a boyfriend back home. I have learned to ask up front if there is a husband or boyfriend in her life!

After Dad died, I went into a deep depression. My regular medications didn't seem to work. On three occasions, I felt so overwhelmed with negative thoughts that I wanted to kill myself. I spent three different times in psychiatric hospitals. In hindsight, I think I was being oppressed by demonic forces.

Each time I called 911, the first question I was asked was, "Do you feel suicidal?" I answered that I did. Soon after one of these calls, an ambulance came, put me in handcuffs and took me to the hospital. Psychiatric hospitals aren't pretty. I was sedated upon arrival. Because I was considered an adult according to my age, I was therefore responsible for myself. My mom was never notified as to my whereabouts and didn't learn of my situation until three days after my admission. She was contacted by someone at JPUSA reporting me missing.

When a person is admitted to a psychiatric ward, their wallet and any emergency information is removed and put in a locker. And I was put on a drug that knocked me out. I couldn't and didn't think to call Mom. The practice at the hospital is to keep the patient for a week, observe him on a new drug and then release him. No contact was made with my current psychiatrist to find out what medications I was on. After my release, I went off the hospital drugs and back onto my former drugs. The whole experience was very frustrating.

There's more! The HIPPA[1] policy doesn't serve the patient or the patient's family. As an adult, I had to give my

1. Health Information Privacy Protection Act.

permission to whomever to know what was happening to me. But, being doped up, my brain wasn't thinking about contacting anyone outside the hospital. I will say that some hospitals are better than others. I have avoided calling 911 for the past several years!

No matter what the circumstances and regardless of how big our problems seem, we can pray and trust that God will give us guidance, strength, and wisdom to carry on. God is bigger than any problem or temptation that Satan may put before us. We can call on the Lord and he will come to our rescue and protect us.

When I was younger, I was frustrated because I felt I was always in my father's shadow. I compared myself to him and realized that I could never be like him. He was good at almost everything he did and was liked and respected by many people. It took years for me to accept the reality that God had made me with different gifts and abilities. God wasn't comparing me to my dad. It was time for me to accept myself.

Dad and I were made with different personalities. Our strengths and weaknesses differ. We are individuals who are uniquely equipped to accomplish what God has planned for our lives. I have learned that I am able to encourage folks who struggle with depression because I understand their emotional needs.

I listen to the Bible on CD when I am in a black mood and need comfort. As I listen, I hear many of the verses that Dad often quoted during his sermons. My dad was my pastor so I heard him quote Scripture every Sunday. As a young Christian, Dad had memorized many Bible verses. In tough times, these verses can bring good counsel and comfort. "Thy word is a lamp to my feet and a light to my path" (Psalm 119:105).

One day, I was in a negative mood and feeling that I was a freak of nature—a mistake. That night, Dad came to me in a dream. I told him that I was sorry for all the grief I had caused him because I had been born a "freak." Dad scolded me and told me that I was not a freak. He said that he wouldn't trade me for a thousand "normal kids." He said that I had a gentle spirit and a deep understanding of people who were suffering. Some so-called "normal" kids never develop these abilities. I was different but in a good way different.

"David, because of your learning disabilities, you have had to work much harder than the other students in order to learn what comes easily for them. You worked hard and didn't give up. We all wish we were different. Hopefully, we come to accept who we are and are thankful for our uniqueness." My dad always had the right words of love and comfort.

24

All Things Work Together
for Good . . .

My RELATIONSHIP with my dad has become more meaningful since his death. Whenever I feel lonely or depressed, he visits me in my dreams and assures me that I have many friends who care for me. When I really miss him, I tell him that I would rather just go to be with him in heaven. Of course, I can't decide when this will occur. Dad reminds me that I am young and have important things to do with my life. He tells me that leaving life isn't the answer for my loneliness. God wants me to make meaningful connections with friends.

I made an earlier reference to this life as the "shadowlands" before our real life begins. Take the example of the caterpillar that starts life as a creepy crawly being. After the pupa stage, a wonderful creature emerges and is able to fly. All of us have the potential to be transformed into someone who can break away from earlier limitations. Sometimes I wish that Dad could see the changes that God is enabling in my life. Then I realize that Dad is seeing them!

Dad appeared to me recently and told me not to grieve or be sad that he had died. Death is simply a transition from the life we know into the life to come. "When I was with you, my life was great, but it was infected with illness, pain, and sin. Now I am here in heaven and my new life is better than I could have imagined. Physical pain is gone as well as disappointments and depression. I no longer have the overwhelming desire to do things my way. Sin is not an issue or a temptation.

"It will be the same for you, David. There will be things for you to do in your life. When it is time for you to come to be with me, all you disabilities—mental, emotional, physical, and spiritual—will be gone! Let what I have said be encouraging to you and keep on plugging away."

Obeying God isn't always easy. Often he will challenge us to do something that is bigger than we can accomplish on our own. Then we must seek the help of others. Life doesn't come prepackaged. It is a messy and inefficient affair. Some of life's hardest lessons come when we bang up against our limitations. Accepting these limitations is a process.

Thankfully, my parents weren't always accepting. When I was diagnosed as having severe emotional issues, my parents didn't accept the psychiatrist's grim diagnosis. He had told my folks that the best thing for me was to put me into a mental institution. After much prayer, my parents decided to keep me at home. I was tutored one-on-one by several teachers. This proved to be the right course. Without distraction, I was able to focus and learn.

When I was older, I discovered my dad's prayer journals. Being a curious youth, I began to read them. The more I read about what the doctor had said about my condition and prognosis, the safer I felt in my parents love for me. Dad had written a plea to God that I wouldn't have to be sent away to an institution. Looking back, I thank God that my parents didn't give in and follow the doctor's advice.

I believe that God gives the parents of special kids an added amount of grace and understanding. At least this was true in my case. I would never have come as far as I have without the loving discipline of my parents. Just because a person is disabled doesn't mean that he or she is unworthy. My parents have a special love for me because I am their son and the result of their love for each other. Christian parents have the added bonus of having God's Holy Spirit living within them, directing them in all their decisions and choices.

25

Acceptance

EVERY YEAR on the anniversary of Dad's birthday or his death, I would become depressed. I am thankful now that I no longer grieve. God is teaching me to be happy about the years that he gave me with my dad. I know that Dad wouldn't want me to be sad. He would want me to celebrate life, rejoicing with my family and friends. Grieving is a process, but eventually we should stop feeling sorry for ourselves and accept the realities of life.

My mom and sister have encouraged me along the way. They have reminded me that friends and family have surrounded me with prayer. Now I can finally see the wisdom in what my family has been telling me. When I allow myself to be overcome with grief, I become my own worst enemy.

It is a hard challenge losing a loving parent, especially one with whom you had a strong, close relationship. I am thankful for having so many friends who showed their concern and love following Dad's death. There is a time for crying, but that time passes and it is time to move on. When a Christian dies, death doesn't end that person's "life." Their "life" will continue in heaven. When I die, I will be reunited with my dad.

A person can have a rich life if he looks to the positive and sees challenges as opportunities for growth. So too, character is built by dealing with heartaches and seemingly impossible problems. Just as strong muscles develop through strength training, maintaining a positive attitude allows for the strength to overcome barriers and limitations. As it says in the 1999 major motion picture, *Galaxy Quest*, "Never give up; never surrender." One day, God will beam me up to be with him!

God brings only good things into our lives. He is not the author of evil. Even in what he allows, he has an ultimate plan that is for our good. All things work together for good, and we know that God causes all things to work together for those who love him.

And there you have it!

Biography and Family Memories of John Bray

THE PUBLIC record tells us John S. Bray was born in Detroit, Michigan, in 1936. The first in his family to go to college, he earned a BA in Philosophy from Wayne State University in Michigan, a Master of Divinity from Fuller Theological Seminary, an MA and PhD in History from Stanford University, and did graduate research in historical theology in Strasbourg, Germany, and Geneva, Switzerland.

He was married to Eleanor Lay in 1969, adopted her daughter, Elizabeth, and had a son, David. An ordained pastor in the Evangelical Covenant Church (ECC), John served as pastor of Salina Covenant Church (Kansas, 1974–1978), Pasadena Covenant Church (California, 1978–1985), and Marin Covenant Church in San Rafael, California (1985–1993). He also served six years on the ECC Executive Board.

Dr. Bray also taught history and philosophy on the faculty at Florida State University (1966-1970), Wayne State College in Nebraska (1970-1974), and he taught part time at Marymount College (1974-1976), Kansas Wesleyan University (1976-1978), and Fuller Theological Seminary (1980-1985). In 1993 he returned to the Midwest to serve for three years as the ninth dean of North Park Theological Seminary in Chicago, until stepping down for health reasons. As professor of church history, he taught until his death from a massive heart attack at age 64. The December 3, 2000, obituary in the *Chicago Tribune* concludes: "John was a mentor to many, a man of God, with a phenomenal intellect and a gentle spirit. He will be remembered as a devoted husband, father, Pastor, teacher and friend." These words point us to the fact that John Bray's life consisted of so much more than the public record.

His sister, Carol, relates their early family life: When John was born, our parents lived in a very small apartment over a bar where Mom worked as a waitress. My brother John slept in a dresser drawer until he got too big for it. When I was born a year later, I took over the drawer. Eventually, our family moved to a one-bedroom flat on Hobart Street in a slum of Detroit. Baby Billy came along and took over the dresser drawer; John slept on a rollaway bed; Bill, Mom, and I shared the one, small bedroom; Dad slept on the sofa in the living room. There was a small bathroom but no shower. Our flat was always kept very clean even though we lived in a poor neighborhood.

John's first job was as a Detroit *Times* newspaper delivery boy. He walked the whole route, carrying the bag of papers on his back or hauling them in his wagon. He always got good tips because he was very dependable. When we weren't working, we played outside: marbles, wall ball, kick-the-can, hide and seek, tag, running races, and cops and robbers. We didn't have a TV set, so the only time we played inside was when it rained or snowed. John won almost any game because he was very smart.

Around the time John was thirteen, he got involved with several local churches in our neighborhood. He made friends from different neighborhoods and knew what kind of life he wanted in his future. John was a great student and turned out to be a great big brother. He worked very hard for his education and we ended up being very close. He was a man who beat the odds. Many of his male friends and cousins ended up on the wrong side of the law. John was the first in our family to go to college. And he didn't stop there. He ended up with a PhD from Stanford and a Master of Divinity from Fuller Seminary. Way to go, Bro! I still miss you.

Libby's stories about her adoptive father echo Carol's ad-miration: When Dad was growing up, his dad told him that he would never amount to anything. My dad showed him! His father was a baker and his mother worked the night shift at the Ford Motor Company. Dad attended Houghton College in New York state but came home when his dad was diagnosed with cancer. At home, Dad attended Wayne State University. Dad was teaching at Florida State University during the time he was working on his dissertation. He was so poor that he had only one suit jacket, which he repaired with his stapler! But he had a variety of ties to "expand his wardrobe." Dad told us that as a boy he played poker for money with the neighborhood guys. And his stories of Stanford pranks were legend.

I first met Dad when Mom and I were living in Wayne, Pennsylvania, with my three cousins. Dad was visiting on his way home from studying in Europe. There was a do-mestic airline strike and he needed a temporary place to stay. At the time, Mom was going through a divorce and was living with her sister and family. My cousins called Dad "Uncle John." That became my name for him until he and Mom married. He later legally adopted me and I became officially his daughter. When Mom married Dad, we moved to where he was teaching in Tallahassee, Florida; shortly after, we packed our stuff along with Dad's sixty boxes of books and moved to Nebraska; four years later, to Kansas, then California.

Dad loved to listen to classical music. Bach was his favorite composer. Dad also enjoyed the Beatles, Simon and Garfunkel, the Bee Gees, and other contemporary groups. Dad had a dry sense of humor, a serious nature, a pastor's heart, and an amazing mind. He seemed to be able to think on several tracks at once. He had many hobbies: stamp collecting, coins, watching sci-fi movies, and looking at fine crystal and gemstones in the stores in the mall. His favorite color was blue, which matched his blue eyes. Dad was smart and yet humble. He had succeeded to escape from the ghetto but never forgot his roots. He modeled God's love for us.

David concludes: Where would I be if my dad had never become a Christian? He, like many of his young adult friends, might have ended up in prison, but for the persistence of a kind neighbor on Hobart Street in Detroit. A refrigeration repairman befriended Dad and invited him to attend church with him. Dad politely declined, but the neighbor continued to offer an invitation. Finally, Dad agreed to attend one Sunday. There he was confronted by the message that there was a God who loved him. Dad continued to attend that church. Later on, he decided to attend Fuller Seminary in order to find answers for his questions about Christianity. Study at Fuller was the launching pad for my dad's future direction in life.

I am forever grateful to that repairman who took an interest in my dad. It is said that children imitate their parents. I am glad that my parents taught me through word and example how to be a Christian man and the importance and effectiveness of prayer. I am grateful for all the folks who have nurtured me in my Christian faith.

Several times when Dad has appeared to me in dreams, he has complimented me on what I have written in this book. It makes me happy that I can honor him in this way. I continue to hope that I will become more and more like him.

www.ingramcontent.com/pod-product-compliance
Lightning Source LLC
Chambersburg PA
CBHW052102270326
41931CB00012B/2853